C000174242

Irish Whiskey Guide

First published in 2009 by
Appletree Press Ltd
The Old Potato Station
14 Howard Street South
Belfast BT7 1AP

Tel: +44 (028) 90 24 30 74
Fax: +44 (028) 90 24 67 56
Email: reception@appletree.ie
Web: www.appletree.ie

Copyright © Appletree Press, 2009
Text by Peter Mulryan
Photographs as acknowledged on p96

A catalogue record for this book is available from the British Library.

Irish Whiskey Guide

ISBN-13: 978 1 84758 120 4

Desk and Marketing Editor: Jean Brown
Copy-editor: Jim Black
Designer: Stuart Wilkinson
Production Manager: Paul McAvoy

9 8 7 6 5 4 3 2 1

AP3602

Please drink sensibly and in moderation

Irish Whiskey Guide

Peter Mulryan

Seo do shláinte! - Here's health!

Contents

A drink precedes a story – Irish Proverb

Preparing Irish Coffee

Introduction

Pocket books are great. You can shove them in your suitcase, bag or even pocket. You can bring them with you to the off licence, the duty free shop or even the supermarket. You can cover them in notes, questions and observations. They can answer idle questions, settle post-dinner party arguments or launch you on a life-long quest to learn more. What's more if a pocket book is lost, stolen or given away, it can easily be replaced for less than the cost of a coffee and a bagel.

So grab this book with both hands and use it as you would a road map. Bring it with you to the pub, choose something different and give your taste buds a treat. If it sparks your imagination there's a lot more to learn, if not then I can heartily recommend it as a coaster. Quite simply Irish whiskey is made to enjoy, so let this book be your introduction to the great tastes and flavours in the spirit of Ireland.

Sláinte,
Peter Mulryan

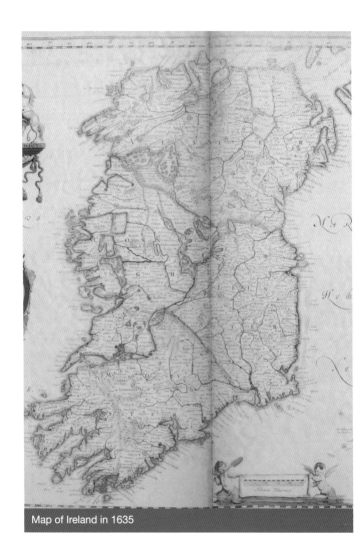
Map of Ireland in 1635

The History of Irish Whiskey

The Early Days

The art of distillation is very ancient: historical records dating from the early Middle Ages describe the Moors' first use of pot-stills to strip essential oils from herbs and plants. The science of distilling is so simple and pure that over the intervening centuries very little has changed. Nowadays stills are made from copper rather than clay, and the spirit goes on to become whiskey and not a perfume or tincture. But the devil is in the detail, and modern whiskey making in Ireland is equal parts science and art.

When distillation started in Ireland is impossible to say, but in all probability it arrived around the same time as a less welcome visitor, the Black Death. The monks, who were the healers of their day, took over where the Moors left off and almost certainly used spirit as a base for medicines, rubs and liniments. Why wouldn't they? Here was a substance as clear as water, that burned like fire and literally preserved flesh. It was nothing less

ELIZABETH.

Queen Elizabeth I was known to be fond of 'uisce beatha'

than the fabled *Water of Life* itself; *Uisce Beatha*. The Irish words were eventually corrupted to give us *Whiskey*.

The *Red Book of Ossory* dating from the early 16th century records uisce beatha being produced for consumption, but the art remained the preserve of the religious Orders. In fact it is not until the Dissolution of the Monasteries in the Tudor period that whiskey ceases to be the drink of the elite. In fact Queen Elizabeth I was known to be fond of the beverage, and she wasn't alone. No less a person than Peter the Great, Czar of Russia, mentioned that "of all wines, the Irish spirit is the best".

With the Tudor settlement of Ireland after the Flight of the Irish Earls, English began to replace native Irish, or Brehon Law. Up until 1607 home distillation was quite legal. However the Crown needed cash and so was anxious to start extracting revenues from the recently settled lands in the Countie of Coleraine. At the time it was common practice for the Crown to lease the

Irish Pub Window

rights or the *patent* to a particular activity, like beer- or whiskey making. For an agreed fee and over an agreed period (usually seven years) the patentee was authorised to realise whatever they could from the area of their licence. One of the first of these licences was issued in 1608 to Sir Thomas Phillips, no less than the deputy to Sir Arthur Chichester, Lord Deputy of Ireland. The area covered was The Route, roughly where the modern town of Bushmills can be found today.

By the middle of the 16th century the corrupt patent system was close to collapse: more cash strapped than ever, the English Crown had to come up with a new way of raising revenue. The modern concept of Excise was born and in 1661 two new drinks were created: tax-paid *Parliament Whiskey* and whiskey on which tax was not paid, which became known as *Poteen*.

By the early part of the 19th century Irish distilling was no longer a cottage industry

The Victorian Heyday

The whiskey industries in Ireland and Scotland went their separate ways early in their development. In Ireland mixed-grain Pot Whiskey was historically the favoured drink, while the Scots traditionally distilled Single Malt. In Ireland the flavour profile of whiskey has historically come from the quality of the raw ingredients. So Irish pot still whiskey was made with unpeated malt, smoke reek not being necessary as the combination of malted and unmalted grain is very flavoursome. This tradition then carried over into the manufacture of Malt Whiskey, with very few Irish malt whiskeys featuring peat in their flavour profile.

The Irish – not their cousins the Scots – were the ones to bring whiskey to the masses. By the early part of the 19th century Irish distilling was no longer a cottage industry. It had mushroomed into a massive industry with the major Dublin distilleries dwarfing anything in Scotland.

The secret of Ireland's success was it could produce a palatable whiskey on a consistent and

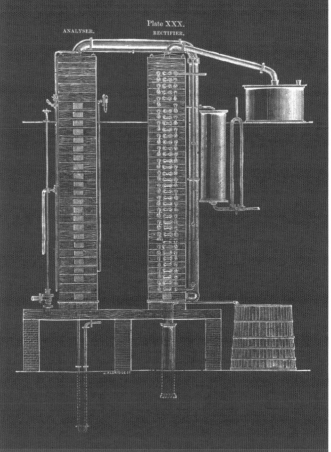

ANALYSER.   Plate XXX.   RECTIFIER.

Irishman Aeneas Coffey perfected a new type of still and patented it in 1831. it revolutionized the whole industry.

sustainable basis. Large orders could be met and shipped around the world, meaning that someone buying a bottle of John Jameson's whiskey could rest assured that it was quality, and that this quality didn't waver. This is in stark contrast to the situation in Scotland, where small farm distilleries produced relatively small quantities of whisky that was of varying quality.

This situation was altered by a new still design, patented by an Irishman. Aeneas Coffey was the former head of Excise in Ireland, a man who knew a thing or two about whiskey. His revolutionary continuous still could produce, in a week, what a traditional pot still would take nine months to make. Though lighter in taste than any whiskey produced at the time, the spirit produced was plentiful and consistent. It also gave distillers huge economies of scale. But the whiskey it made was famously bland – it was derided by the Irish distillers of the time as "silent spirit". Coffey turned his back on Ireland and moved to Scotland. Here in Scotland's industrial central belt huge distilleries produced massive amounts

Commissioner for New York watches as agents pour whiskey into the sewers during Prohibition

of Mr Coffey's silent spirit. They then mixed this light spirit with pungent Highland Malt, to create something altogether new – the Blended whisky we know today. This drink would revolutionise the industry in Scotland and give the world a new drink. "Scotch" brands like Johnnie Walker, Haig and Vat 69 took the world by storm and the Irish industry suffered.

During the 19th century, the main Irish whiskey producers were engaged in lucrative export trade with America, England and its colonies, including India, Australia and Canada. The late 19th and early 20th centuries defined a very difficult period for the whiskey industry in Ireland. By failing to adopt whiskey blending, which the distillers of Scotch had embraced from the 1880s, the Irish industry slowly lost its predominant position. This major problem was added to by the loss of Colonial markets during the wars of Independence and the economic war with Britain. Prohibition in America during 1929-1932 also had a negative effect on Irish whiskey sales.

Back from the Brink

By the middle of the 20th century the Irish whiskey industry had been brought to its knees, by a mixture of arrogance and bad luck. To survive, let alone prosper, Irish whiskey would need the one thing it had been lacking for close to a century: leadership.

In 1966, the three remaining distillers in the Republic of Ireland: Jameson, Powers and Cork Distillers Company merged to form a new group, Irish Distillers. This radical move would involve closing the three existing distilleries, two in Dublin and one in Cork, and moving all production to a new facility in Midleton, County Cork.

During the 1980s, after decades in the doldrums the Irish whiskey industry started to claw its way back on to the world stage. Irish Distillers picked Jameson to be their standard bearer, and after the takeover of that company by Pernod Ricard, Irish whiskey finally found its feet. In 1987 John Teeling established Ireland's first new distillery for over a century: Cooley focused on producing malt whiskey. Some twenty years after its foundation it won 2008's World Distiller of the Year Award. Long a part of Irish Distillers, Ireland's oldest working distillery, Old Bushmills was taken over by Diageo in 2005, giving the Irish industry another shot in the arm.

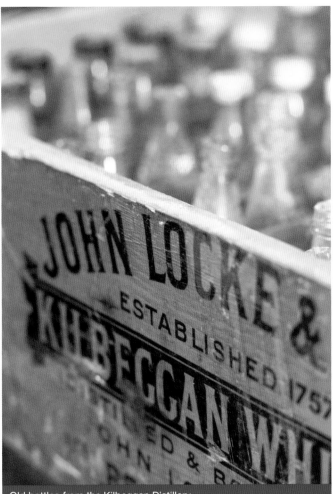
Old bottles from the Kilbeggan Distillery

Types of Irish Whiskey

In order to be called *Irish Whiskey*, the spirit in question has to be produced on the island of Ireland, be distilled from grain and be matured for no less than three years in oak casks. Irish whiskey cannot be sold at anything less than 40 per cent alcohol by volume (ABV).

But as you would expect from a drink as old and as fine as Irish whiskey, there is a lot more to this spirit than a simple classification.

Four types of whiskey are produced in Ireland: grain whiskey; single malt, pure pot still whiskey and blended whiskey.

Grain Whiskey

Grain whiskey is produced in a continuous still from corn or maize. It is a light and fragrant spirit and rarely seen out on its own as it's usually blended with malt whiskey or pure pot still to gives us best-selling blends like Jameson, Black Bush or Kilbeggan. However Cooley Distillery have bottled two versions of their single grain Greenore; the 8-Year-Old is very tasty indeed while the 15-Year-Old is truly spectacular.

Single Malt

A single malt is just that: a whiskey made from malted barley and produced at a single distillery.

The vast majority of Irish Malt Whiskey comes from just two distilleries. Old Bushmills in County Antrim and the Cooley distillery in County Louth between them produce a huge selection of fabulous whiskeys. Ireland's largest distillery at Midleton in County Cork also produces a single malt, however this is almost impossible to get hold of as it is usually kept for blending purposes. The last time Malt from Midleton came up for sale was in the USA when bottled as "Erin go Bragh" (Ireland forever). If you ever see a bottle buy two – one for you and one for me.

Midleton distillery is however the only plant in the country to produce Pure Pot Still Whiskey.

Pure Pot Still

A malt whiskey then is one made from malt; that is sprouted barley. Traditionally however the favoured Irish spirit was always made from a combination of malted *and* unmalted barley, a mix called 'pot still whiskey'. Unmalted barley gives traditional Irish pot still a very different taste and mouth feel to malt whiskey. Pot still whiskeys are large, fat and almost oily. At one time just about every Irish whiskey was a pure pot still whiskey, but the appellation almost disappeared in the 1970s as Irish Distillers reformulated all their brands. Today there are just two brands left on sale – Green Spot and Redbreast.

Blended Whiskey

Blends are the unsung heroes of the Irish whiskey world. Brands like Jameson, Paddy, Powers, Black Bush, Locke's and Kilbeggan sell in vast quantities, but are mostly taken for granted by consumers. A 'blend' is quite simply a blend of grain whiskey with either malt or pot still, or sometimes all three.

How Irish Whiskey is Made

Irish whiskey is made from three simple ingredients: water, barley and yeast. Many would argue that of the three, barley is the most important.

Barley

Barley can be either malted or unmalted. We say that grain is malted when it is soaked in water and allowed to germinate, which gives us *green malt*.

So *malt whiskey* then, is made from 100 per cent malted barley. *Pot still whiskey* is made from a mixture of malted and unmalted barley.

Both *malt-* and *pot still* whiskey are made in batches in traditional copper pot stills.

Malting

Malting is the process that helps convert the barley starch into sugar, and it is this sugar that will eventually get turned into alcohol by the yeast.

Barley is an essential ingredient in the creation of both whiskey and beer

Grinding the green malt into grist

Barley is malted by letting it sprout, then stopping the germination with heat. If the heat comes from peat smoke, then the whiskey will have a tell-tale smoky taste like that found in Connemara. Alternatively, the heat can come from warm air, which does not flavour the whiskey: this is the type of barley used at Old Bushmills.

Grist

The green malt (or a mixture of green malt and barley if pot still whiskey is being produced) is ground into a coarse flour called *grist* and dumped into a large tub known as a *mash tun or kieve*. Hot water is added and the mixture is stirred to help convert the starch in the grain into sugar.

This process is repeated three times, with the barley water being drained off after each mashing. The final wash is held and used in the first mashing of the next batch of grist, ensuring a certain continuity between batches.

Fermenting

The sweet *wort* is the raw material from which whiskey will be made. However it is a two-stage process: before it becomes whiskey, the wort must get turned into a kind of beer. Yeast is added to the wort, and the murky liquid starts to bubble and foam as the sugars get to work and start to generate alcohol.

Distilling

When the wort calms down, most of the sugar has been digested by the yeast and the ugly duckling beer is ready for its transformation. Suitably the copper pot stills that work their magic have elegant swan necks. Here the wort is heated until the alcohol vaporises: it is cooled, collected and distilled a second time in the case of Cooley, a third time in the case of both Midleton and Bushmills.

Maturation

The final spirit that flows from the stills is clear as water. It will be at least three years before it can be called whiskey, and during that time the

Hot water is added to the grist in a mash tun

Jameson Whiskey maturing

spirit will be maturing in oak barrels. Most of these casks will have previously held bourbon or sherry, though some rum and cognac casks, port pipes and even virgin wood are used.

It is the complex interaction between whiskey and wood which gives Irish malt whiskeys so much of their flavour. It is also the part of the process about which we know the least. Nature it would seem is slow to give up her secrets.

Old Bushmills Distillery dammed St Columb's Rill so that there is a constant water supply for all their processes

The Influences on Malt Whiskey

Production:

Water

As an island with a temperate climate, it is not surprising to learn that Ireland is blessed with a plentiful supply of water. This is just as well as water is vital to the whole whiskey making process – so crucial in fact, that at Old Bushmills they have dammed their supply. The small lake formed by St Columb's Rill not only provides ducks with somewhere to swim, and photographers with great shots, but most importantly ensures that the distillery will never run short of water, as it is used in just about every stage of the distilling process.

All of Ireland's distilleries monitor their water supplies and go to extreme lengths to ensure they remain clean and pure. After all the water used to make Irish whiskey is not treated in any way, just filtered before use.

Locke's Distillery used wild yeast during the 1940s

However important water is in the whiskey making process, it is not critical to the favour profile of Irish malt whiskey. There are a couple of reasons for this. Firstly the water used is very pure and therefore neutral in taste. Secondly and more crucially, the various distilling regimes used by all three Irish distilleries are so radically different, that they have much more impact on taste than water ever could. At Old Bushmills for example, all whiskeys are triple distilled, while those at Cooley are distilled twice.

Yeast

Without yeast there would be no beer, bread or whiskey. It is remarkable stuff and it is everywhere. In the 1940s Locke's Distillery in the Midlands used to leave wild yeasts go to work on the wort. I have seen modern Tequila plants in Mexico do the same; they just leave their wort exposed to the air and eventually the yeasts that make apples rot and cheese turn to fur will get to work and the process of fermentation will begin.

Relying on wild yeasts is however a very inexact science, especially as along with producing alcohol and carbon dioxide, yeasts also leave behind numerous compounds like acids and esters that in turn add flavour to the wash. Nowadays all Irish distilleries use commercial yeasts – they go out of their way to exclude their wild cousins.

Barley

Wheat and corn can be used to make the cheap grain whiskeys that bulk out blends, but to make a decent malt you need the king of cereals – barley.

Barley is hardy stuff and it grows well in our damp northern climate. Its ability to thrive on almost any soil made it a reliable cash crop for farmers. To this day barley can be seen growing all across the island of Ireland.

Distilling was traditionally a seasonal activity, kicking off in the late autumn with swollen rivers to power the plant, and grain stores heaving with the recently harvested spring barley. As the

To make a decent malt you need the king of cereals – barley

Cutting turf in the Maamturk Mountains near Cong. It has been used as fuel for generations.

distilling season began to extend to cover most of the year, so strains of winter barley were slowly introduced. Today they account for around half of Midleton's barley needs.

Cooley stands alone in Ireland in that it uses both peated and unpeated malt. Dried over a peat fire, the malt imparts its smoky, peaty character onto the end malt.

The level of peating is expressed as parts per million (ppm) of phenols. Cooley set their level at 15ppm, which is low in comparison to some Scottish distilleries, but that doesn't stop their peated whiskeys from delivering quite a punch.

Copper

Copper is curious stuff. It has the lustre of gold, it conducts heat beautifully and when warm it feels almost alive. It is not surprising therefore that copper is so often worked into pots, pans and pot stills.

Copper pot stills at Old Bushmills Distillery

What is most fascinating about copper though is that it is "soft". In other words, every wash that goes through a copper pot still takes some of the copper with it. So copper plays a huge part in shaping the flavour of Irish whiskey, which it does in many ways.

Walk into any Irish distillery and you will see the massive copper pot stills reaching proudly for the sky. It is in these stills that the element gets to play an essential role in the alchemy of distilling. The copper in the stills reacts with the spirit being produced, neutralising "bad" components and giving a piece of itself up to every distillation. Over the course of decades the stills thin, to the point that they have to be replaced. When this happens distillers make sure that the replacement is as near identical to the original as possible.

Man Made:

Nature gives us the raw ingredients and we turn them into whiskey: that is all we do. The way we make whiskey today is not radically different from the way it has always been done. We use computers and nowadays pot stills are heated with steam, but the laws of physics do not change – all we have done is streamline the process. The trades and the skills that were in demand a century ago are still in demand today. How many industries can you say that about?

At the heart of each bottle of Irish Malt are a group of highly trained and highly committed individuals.

Maltster

These days Maltsters do not work in the distillery, they work in dedicated Malt Houses. But the skills they employ are as crucial as ever. If the barley is not malted to perfection, everything else is a waste of time. The knowledge of how long to soak the barley, when to stop the process of germination and exactly how long to dry the grain cannot be mechanised. Computers cannot tell from touch just how much water a handful of barley has soaked up, and they certainly cannot chew on some malt and know from the taste alone that their work is done.

Distiller

The Distiller is a master of many skills, orchestrating everything, from day-to-day operations, through quality control to gazing into the future. Think about it: whiskey has to be at least three years old before it can be sold, but in fact most Irish whiskey is sold when considerably older. Whiskey stocks cannot be magicked out of thin air – someone has to plan what will be needed a decade or more into the future. It is not an exact science: getting it wrong can cost dearly; getting it right means that future demand can be met. The entire distilling process must be directed with almost instinctive skill and judgement. The job of the Master Distiller then is one of the most demanding in this already highly skilled industry.

Stillman

The Stillman is the person who does the day-to-day distilling. They have to make all the tough operational decisions. A wrong call can ruin an entire batch of whiskey, as they decide when to collect spirit and when to stop. This is how distilleries produce lighter or heavier malts, with the former coming from the more central portion

The skill of the cooper is to keep the whisky safe in a barrel

of the run. Letting things run too far however produces whiskey that tastes like old damp raincoats. Not very pleasant.

Cooper

Once hundreds of Coopers tapped out a living in Ireland's numerous breweries and distilleries. Before the advent of stainless steel, wooden casks were used not only for maturation, but also for transportation.

Irish Whiskey is matured in oak casks: some are new but the vast majority have previously been used to mature either Scottish or American whiskey. New casks can be quite assertive, so one that has had a previous occupant tends to be best, as it won't overwhelm the subtle flavours of Irish Malt. A bad cask can ruin a batch of whiskey, while a leaky one can be almost as expensive. The skill of the Cooper is to keep the whiskey safe in a barrel made of sound timber – it may well be in the wood for several decades, so it is a job worth doing properly.

Whisky maturing at Locke's Distillery

Maturation:

Time

Time cannot be hurried, so it is no wonder that a Victorian invention, which boasted it could age whiskey more rapidly, never caught on. You cannot speed up time, and the years and decades that a whiskey lies in wood are crucially important.

As it ages Malt Whiskey evaporates through the porous wood, at the rate of 2 per cent of volume per year. This is called the "angels' share" as the only ones who can appreciate it as it spirals skyward are the angels. There aren't many industries where a product is produced, left for a decade or more while it gets smaller and smaller, before being eventually sold. But that is the way it has to be with Irish Malt, because the one thing you cannot hurry is time.

Wood

The wooden casks into which the malt is filled have to be chosen carefully. The wood has to be oak, and whiskey makers are very fussy as to

Casks just filled with newly-made Bushmills spirit

where their casks come from. Irish distilleries have relationships with distillers on both sides of the Atlantic, and with sherry houses in Jerez, Spain.

Bottles of fine Irish Malt Whiskey carry an age statement for a reason. Time is an expensive commodity: it cannot be bought, so whiskey distillers are at pains not to waste it. The age statement refers to the youngest whiskey contained in each bottle.

Climate

Climate is the final variable that affects the taste of Irish Malt Whiskey. As a general rule of thumb, the warmer the weather the faster the spirit will age. Whiskey therefore matures more slowly in Scotland than in Ireland, and more slowly in Ireland than in Tennessee.

No two Irish malt whiskeys taste the sa

Enjoyment of Irish Whiskey

The Malts of Ireland

No two Irish malt whiskeys taste the same. Some like Tyrconnell are light and fruity, others such as Old Bushmills 10-Year-Old are malty and approachable, while more like Connemara Cask Strength have huge character and really make their presence felt. New bottlings come and go all the time – some from the distillery, some from independent bottlers – but the following list will do very well as a starting point.

Old Bushmills

There have been numerous Distillery malt bottlings over the years, especially in the late 1980s and early 1990s, all now discontinued. The bottling you are most likely to stumble across is a 5-Year-Old Bushmills Malt, destined for the Italian market.

Around the Millennium, Bushmills produced a series of single cask bottlings, from a selection of Bourbon, Rum and Sherry wood all typically

10-Year-Old Single Malt from the Old Bushmills Distillery

around 14 years old. With no age statement, this programme has now been discontinued. The last bottling was a 1993 Single Cask Bottling for La Maison du Whisky in France: all of these expressions are now very collectable.

Bushmills Malt 10-Year-Old

This is the standard against which all other Irish Malts are measured. The 10-Year-Old Bushmills malt is matured mainly in ex-Bourbon casks, with just a small proportion of Sherry casks added for good measure. This is a very drinkable classy malt, unique in that it appeals equally to the novice whiskey drinker and the malt whiskey fancier. Not an easy task!

Bushmills Malt 16-Year-Old

This expression of Antrim Malt is made up in equal proportion of 16-Year-Old Bushmills Malt from Sherry casks and Bourbon casks. These are married together then re-casked in ex-Port pipes, typically for 6-9 months of extra maturation. This in the trade is called "finishing".

FROM THE WORLD'S OLDEST WHISKEY DISTILLERS
ORIGINAL GRANT
TO DISTIL
1608

BUSHMILLS
MALT
21
AGED — YEARS
RARE

Matured in Three Woods

The Old Bushmills Distillery Co. Ltd

SINGLE MALT

21-Year-Old Bushmills Single Malt

The result is a complex firecracker of a malt, with loads of dried fruit character adding sweetness to the malty whiskey. Exceptional.

Bushmills Malt 21-Year-Old

This unusual malt shows just how crucial wood is in making up the flavour of a decent Malt. Equal proportions of 19-Year-Old Bushmills Malt, from Sherry casks and Bourbon casks, are vatted together then re-casked in ex-Madeira drums for a further 2 years' extra maturation. Less than 10,000 bottles of this Malt are produced every year.

This very complex whiskey offers something different on every visit – a hugely enjoyable malt, and one that silences Scotch whiskey snobs.

Bushmills Malt 12-Year-Old Distillery Reserve

Available only at the County Antrim distillery, this butterscotch malt is produced in very limited quantities and is well worth suitcase space.

Locke's 8-Year-Old Whiskey

Cooley Distillery

This distillery on the Cooley peninsula in County Louth has only been in production since the late 1980s so does not yet have a huge back catalogue of whiskey expressions. However what it lacks there, it more than makes up for it with a huge variety of malt types.

Locke's 8-Year-Old

Until the 1950s Locke's was one of Ireland's favourite whiskeys. Cooley now have a small micro-distillery in the old Locke's distillery in County Westmeath and the name lives on in a variety of bottlings.

The 8-Year-Old is their entry-level malt: it is very lightly peated and pleasantly floral.

Tyrconnell

When it was a shade over 3 years old, a very fragrant and totally peat-free Tyrconnell was the first malt released by Cooley; the original bottlings (complete with three stars on the label) can still be found if you do a bit of searching.

Tyrconnell has a variety of different finishes

This is a wonderfully light, delicate malt, delivering a huge bouquet of boiled sweets on the nose. The whiskey also has crisp body and a malty sweetness that is very drinkable. A very enjoyable malt that is unique and hugely sippable.

Tyrconnell also comes in a range of finishes including Malt finished in Sherry, Port and Madeira wood. The wood finishes complement the floral nature of the malt very well. All three are very attractive, with the Sherry wood winning by a nose.

Connemara

The far west of Ireland, where history and myth collide, is where you will find Connemara. It is not on many maps, but you will know when you get there. Aim for the Galway/Mayo border and you won't go far wrong.

It is a wild land of mountains, streams and bogs, where Nature is very much in control and where at best Man simply survives. It is not too surprising that Cooley named their revolutionary whiskey after this state of mind.

Connemara Peated Single Malt

There had been no peated Irish malt since we don't know when: this was not just a malt, it was a statement. They couldn't afford to screw it up.

The good news is that Cooley pulled it off in style. The Connemara range is quite simply one of the finest innovations in modern whiskey history – a real throwback to the days when men wore funny beards, dressed in tweed and whiskey making was elemental.

The entry-level product is simply called Connemara and it is a real show-stopper. There is no west coast of Scotland iodine here, just west coast of Ireland peat. And lots of it, but at the same time there is a lightness you just don't get on Islay or on Skye. Delicious.

Connemara 12-Year-Old

A little longer in the wood produces a bigger yet more subtle monster. The peat is almost pipe-smoke smooth and the finish is enormous.

Connemara Cask Strength

Whiskey as Nature intended. Big, bold, beautiful.

Green Spot Irish Whiskey

Midleton Distillery

Midleton is Ireland's largest distillery, and the only one to produce traditional pure pot still whiskey. There are two expressions that are readily available.

Green Spot

This label is owned by Mitchell and Son of Dublin, the last Irish whiskey bonders. They buy the pot still from Midleton and sell it as Green Spot, as they have done for four generations.

The whiskey is between 7- and 12 years old and being a pot still is made from a mixture of malted and unmalted barley. This is a cracking adventure of a drink, at once historic, delicious and unique. The unmalted barley gives this whiskey real crackle, best with a few drops of water to unlock the tinderbox of taste.

A 10- and a 12-Year-Old version were released in the early Noughties and some bottles can still be bought, if you have the money.

Redbreast Pure Pot Still Whiskey

Redbreast

Redbreast was originally a label under which Jameson was bottled. Today the brand comes from Midleton and at 15 years old is the most ancient pure pot still whiskey on sale today. Redbreast is in many ways similar to Green Spot, though it is heavier, oilier and has hints of sherry as it is matured for at least 15 years in sherry casks and bourbon barrels. Like all good pot still whiskeys Redbreast is a creature unto itself, quite unlike a Malt in its steely viscosity.

'Here's health and prosperity' – traditional Irish Toast

What to Choose

Like fine wines, there are whiskeys to suit all moods and tastes. Exploring them is a real education. However choosing can sometimes be difficult: here is a guide to start you off.

Five Light Aperitif Malts or Pot Still Whiskeys

Tyrconnell
Bushmills 10-Year-Old
Locke's Single Malt
Bushmills 16-Year-Old
Green Spot

Five Weightier Digestif Malts or Pot Still Whiskeys

Bushmills 21-Year-Old Single Malt
Bushmills 18-Year-Old Single Malt
Connemara Cask Strength
Redbreast
Tyrconnell Sherry Finish

Paddy was named in honour of a legendary salesman

The Blended Whiskeys of Ireland

The vast majority of Irish blends hail from a single source: the giant Midleton distillery in County Cork. This is now home to 'the big three': Jameson, Powers and Paddy. Even the grain whiskey used to make the world-beating Black Bush is distilled to order here, as well as Tullamore Dew.

The other source of blended Irish is the Cooley plant in County Louth. Here all the grain and malt used to make Kilbeggan and Locke's blends is made under the one roof. In fact most of the retailer own-brand Irish you'll find in supermarkets across the globe is made by Cooley.

Powers Gold Label Irish Whiskey

From the Midleton Distillery:

Jameson
The world's largest selling Irish whiskey comes in a variety of ages and styles; the 12-Year-Old is the real winner here.

Powers
Like Jameson, Powers Gold Label was once made in Dublin. It is now the largest selling whiskey in Ireland, and with good reason. Powers is packed full of pot still whiskey and is a real cracker.

Paddy
Lighter in character than Powers, this quite malty dram is a gentle everyday whiskey; there's plenty to enjoy here. Interestingly, Paddy is named after legendary whiskey salesman Paddy Flaherty, stood rounds of his favourite whiskey thus creating a taste and a market for it. Genius!

Tullamore Dew:
Originally from the Irish Midlands, Tullamore Dew is quite grainy and goes well with a mixer whether ginger or soda.

Kilbeggan

From the Bushmills Distillery:

The grain whiskey used in both Bushmills Original and Black Bush is specially made in Midleton, but the malt still comes from County Antrim, where the brands are blended, bottled and matured. Of the two Bushmills blends, Black Bush would be the one to take to a desert island.

From the Cooley Distillery:

All Cooley whiskeys are produced in the County Louth distillery, and matured in the old stone warehouses of Locke's Distillery in the town of Kilbeggan.

Kilbeggan
Kilbeggan is one of Ireland's great secrets, and it knocks the socks off just about everything else in the same price bracket.

Locke's
As well as a Locke's single malt, there is a blend which is thinner than its stablemates but is still good when mixed with cola or ginger.

Millars Special Reserve Irish Whiskey

Inishowen

Unlike any other Irish blend, this whiskey is lightly peated. It is a tasty choice if Scotch whisky is more to your usual taste.

Millars

In a world of bland global whiskey brands, this hard-to-find offering is a wonderful little gem.

Five Brilliant Blends

Jameson 12-Year-Old
Kilbeggan 15-Year-Old
Powers
Black Bush
Millars

Ingredients for a hot whiskey

Malt Whiskey in the Kitchen

Hot Whiskey

"Hot whiskey please" is a call you will hear in just about every Irish pub during the long damp winter. It is warming, welcoming and is often also used to help fight the common cold!

boiling water
slice of lemon
3 cloves
heaped teaspoon of sugar
shot of whiskey

Stud a slice of lemon with three cloves. Put one heaped teaspoon of sugar into the bottom of a heavy glass. Add a teacup of boiling water and stir until the sugar has melted. Add a shot of whiskey and the studded lemon. Stir and enjoy.

Irish Coffee

Irish Coffee

During the glamorous 1940s the only way to cross the Atlantic in style was in a "flying boat". These planes landed in Foynes, near modern-day Shannon airport. One wet night during the Second World War a group of damp American passengers were cheered up when airport barman Joseph Sheridan decided to add some Irish whiskey to their coffee and instantly created a classic.

½ cup hot, strong, black coffee
1 measure of Irish whiskey
1-2 teaspoons of sugar
double or whipped cream

Mix half a cup of good quality coffee with one measure of Irish whiskey, add a spoon or two of sugar and stir. Then float some double or whipped cream on top.

Visitors' centre at Locke's Distillery, Kilbeggan

Visiting Distilleries

John Clement Ryan, the last remaining member of the Powers whiskey family, put whiskey tourism firmly on the map when he pioneered a visitor's centre at the Old Midleton distillery.

Now the whiskey connoisseur and the casual tourist have a whole range of places they can visit. In Midleton you can experience the vast scale of a Victorian plant; in Kilbeggan you can step back in time and see how a small rural operation looked when it closed in the mid-1950s, and at Old Bushmills you can actually walk around a working distillery. There are other centres in Tullamore and Dublin.

Each visitor centre is different and they all celebrate whiskey production and highlight the importance and the uniqueness of Irish whiskey.

JJ's Bar at the Old Jameson Distillery Visitors' Centre

The Old Jameson Distillery, Bow Street Distillery, Smithfield, Dublin 7 – (00 353) 01 807 2355

Tours at the Old Jameson Distillery in Dublin can be taken in numerous languages. This is a huge operation and the complex features shops, bars and restaurants.

The Old Jameson Distillery is open 363 days a year. The first tour commences at 9.30am and tours run until 6pm, the last tour is at 5.30pm. The Irish Whiskey Corner bar opens at 5.30pm until closing time. Open Bank Holidays, but closed Good Friday and over Christmas.

Jameson Heritage Centre, Midleton

The Jameson Heritage Centre, The Old Distillery, Midleton, County Cork – (00 353) 021 461 3594

The modern Midleton distillery, home to Jameson, is tucked behind the magnificent cut stone and red brick Victorian distillery. The new plant is out of bounds, but there is enough in the old distillery to occupy anyone for several hours.

There is also a restaurant, and a shop featuring everything from t-shirts to – not too surprisingly – whiskey.

The Jameson Heritage Centre is open year round, Monday-Sunday. Opening time from March-October is 10am to 5pm, with tours on demand. From November to December tours are daily from 11am, 2.30pm and 4pm.

The Old Bushmills Distillery

Old Bushmills, 2 Distillery Road, Bushmills,
County Antrim BT57 8XH – (0044) 028 2073
3218 / 3272

The Old Bushmills Distillery is unique as the only
operational Irish distillery that accepts visitors.
There is also a small shop where you can
purchase the excellent Distillery Reserve.

This is working distillery, so at times certain parts
may be closed or off-limits to the
tour. The opening hours also vary
enormously depending on the
season. It is best to telephone, but
as a rule of thumb the distillery is
open 7 days a week between 9am
and 5pm with tours available on
demand.

Locke's Distillery Museum, Kilbeggan

Locke's Distillery Museum, Lower Main Street, Kilbeggan, County Westmeath – (00 353) 057 933 2134

This museum is one of the wonders of the Irish industrial landscape. It is pretty much a time capsule capturing life in the rural Ireland of the 1950s, when the plant closed. Run by locals it is unlike many other museums – it still has a real connection with the industry.

Cooley still mature their whiskeys in the century-old warehouses and a small "micro-distillery" was brought into production in 2007, to coincide with the distillery's 150th anniversary.

Locke's Distillery Museum is open from April to October, 9am to 6pm daily, and from November to April from 10am to 4pm daily.

Exhibit at Tullamore Dew Heritage Centre

Tullamore Dew Heritage Centre, Bury Quay, Tullamore, County Offaly – (00 353) 057 932 5015

Whilst distilling no longer takes place in Tullamore, the Tullamore Dew Heritage Centre will take you through the history of the whole area and the development of Tullamore town.

The Centre is located in a four-storey warehouse, which was built on the banks of the Grand Canal for maturing Tullamore Dew Irish Whiskey. You will also find a welcoming bar and shop.

Tullamore Dew Heritage Centre opens from daily May to September 9am to 6pm, and from October to April from 10am to 5pm. Opens Sunday and Bank Holidays from 12 noon to 5pm.

Acknowledgements

The publisher would like to thank the following for permission to reproduce work in copyright:

© istockphoto.com / Soubrette (p4)
© istockphoto.com / inhauscreative (p6)
© istockphoto.com / John W Defeo (p8)
© istockphoto.com / Photo by N Staykov (p10)
© istockphoto.com. / Duncan Walker (p12)
© istockphoto.com / David Shawley (p14)
© istockphoto.com / Varela (p16)
© Diageo Archive (p18)
© Library of Congress. Prints and Photographs Division (p20)
© Cooley Distillery. Photographs by O'Sullivan Photography (p24, 30, 33, 38, 48, 50, 60, 62, 64, 76, 78, 84, 92 and 93)
© istockphoto.com / Chris Scredon (p29)
© Irish Distillers Pernod Ricard (p34, 68, 72, 74, 86, 87, 88, and 89)
© The Old Bushmills Distillery Co. Ltd (p36, 41, 44, 52, 56, 58, 90 and 91)
© istockphoto.com / Phil Augustus (p42)
© istockphoto.com / Ville Ahonen (p54)
© Mitchell and Son Ltd (p66)
© istockphoto.com / my-walkabout.com (p70)
© John Murphy (p80)
© istockphoto.com / Camrocker (p82)
© Tullamore Dew. Photograph by Gary McGivney (p94)
© C&C International (p95)